Drugs and Alcohol

by Ashley Kuehl

Consultant: Caitlin Krieck, Social Studies Teacher and Instructional Coach, The Lab School of Washington

Minneapolis, Minnesota

Credits
Cover and title page, © goodbishop/Shutterstock; 3, © irin-k/Shutterstock; 5, © YinYang/iStock; 7, © ldutko/Shutterstock; 9, © Mike Fig Photo/Shutterstock; 11, © Motortion Films/Shutterstock; 13, © Monkey Business Images/Shutterstock; 15, © AnnaStills/iStock; 17, © Katya Havok/Shutterstock; 19, © Jordi Carne Sanchez/iStock; 21, © Studio Romantic/Shutterstock; 23, © VLADGRIN/iStock; 25, © SDI Productions/iStock; 27, © Monkey Business Images/Shutterstock; 28A, © Thomas Lydell/iStock; 28B, © MOHSHINBD/Shutterstock; 28C, © Sunnydream/Shutterstock; 28D, © Sasha Turkina/Shutterstock

Bearport Publishing Company Product Development Team
Publisher: Jen Jenson; Director of Product Development: Spencer Brinker; Editorial Director: Allison Juda; Editor: Cole Nelson; Editor: Tiana Tran; Production Editor: Naomi Reich; Art Director: Kim Jones; Designer: Kayla Eggert; Designer: Steve Scheluchin; Production Specialist: Owen Hamlin

Statement on Usage of Generative Artificial Intelligence
Bearport Publishing remains committed to publishing high-quality nonfiction books. Therefore, we restrict the use of generative AI to ensure accuracy of all text and visual components pertaining to a book's subject. See BearportPublishing.com for details.

Library of Congress Cataloging-in-Publication Data is available at www.loc.gov or upon request from the publisher.

ISBN: 979-8-89577-073-3 (hardcover)
ISBN: 979-8-89577-520-2 (paperback)
ISBN: 979-8-89577-190-7 (ebook)

Copyright © 2026 Bearport Publishing Company. All rights reserved. No part of this publication may be reproduced in whole or in part, stored in any retrieval system, or transmitted in any form or by any means, electronic, mechanical, photocopying, recording, or otherwise, without written permission from the publisher. Bearport Publishing is a division of FlutterBee Education Group.

For more information, write to Bearport Publishing, 3500 American Blvd W, Suite 150, Bloomington, MN 55431.

Contents

Fiction, Not Fact. 4
What Are Drugs?. 6
Depressants 8
Stimulants. 12
Opioids 14
Hallucinogens 16
Beyond Use to Abuse. 18
Can't Stop 20
Seeking Help 24
Staying Healthy 26

Types of Drugs 28
SilverTips for Success 29
Glossary 30
Read More 31
Learn More Online 31
Index 32
About the Author. 32

Fiction, Not Fact

Have you seen movies where characters drink alcohol? How about shows where someone does other drugs? These kinds of images are all over pop culture. But often, they are not realistic. They don't show the whole story. What is the truth about drugs?

> More than three million people die each year because of alcohol and other kinds of drugs. This makes up almost 5 percent of all deaths around the world.

What Are Drugs?

Drugs are substances that affect the body. Sometimes, they are helpful. Doctors **prescribe** drugs as medicine. They are used to treat sicknesses.

Some people take drugs **recreationally**. They use them because they like how the drugs make them feel. However, this is not always safe. Sometimes, it is **illegal**.

> Taking medicine prescribed by a doctor is legal. In some cases, so is using alcohol, tobacco, and cannabis. However, there are many laws about drugs.

Depressants

Different kinds of drugs affect the body differently. They are grouped into categories.

Depressants (di-PRESS-uhntz) cause the brain and body to slow down. Doctors prescribe them for many reasons. These drugs help people sleep. They can make muscles relax. Some are used to fight **anxiety**.

> Alcohol is a depressant. Cannabis is usually included as part of this group, too. Cannabis is also known as marijuana, weed, and many other names.

Like all drugs, depressants can have **side effects**. Someone using depressants may slur their speech. They might move their body differently. A person's balance can be affected. They may fall.

These drugs also affect thinking. People can get confused. They may make different choices than they would without the drugs.

> People using depressants have more accidents. If they drive, they are more likely to get into crashes.

Stimulants

Stimulants (STIM-yuh-luhntz) can have the opposite effect of depressants. Drugs in this group make the brain and body work faster. People use stimulants to feel more awake.

The extra energy can come with a faster heart rate. Stimulants may also cause shaking or **seizures**. They make some people anxious.

> Caffeine is a legal stimulant. Cocaine and meth are illegal stimulants. All of these drugs can keep people awake.

Caffeine can be found in coffee, tea, and soda.

Opioids

Opioids (OH-pee-*oidz*) are sometimes called painkillers. Drugs in this group attach to **nerves**. They block or lessen the feeling of pain. Doctors may give people opioids to treat pain.

Sometimes, people use opioids without a prescription. This is illegal. It can also be very dangerous.

> Fentanyl (FEN-teh-*nil*) is an extremely strong opioid. Doctors can prescribe it. Sometimes, it gets added to illegal drugs. Fentanyl is responsible for the most **overdoses** in the United States. A small amount can easily turn deadly.

People are sometimes prescribed opioids after surgery.

Hallucinogens

Hallucinogens (huh-LOO-suh-nuh-jenz) are drugs that change how someone senses the world. They can make people see or hear things that aren't real.

Sometimes, these drugs make people feel scared or anxious. Other times, people feel very happy. LSD and magic mushrooms are common hallucinogens.

> Feeling the effects of these drugs is often called tripping. People using hallucinogens cannot control their experience. Some have negative thoughts or see scary things. This is referred to as being on a bad trip.

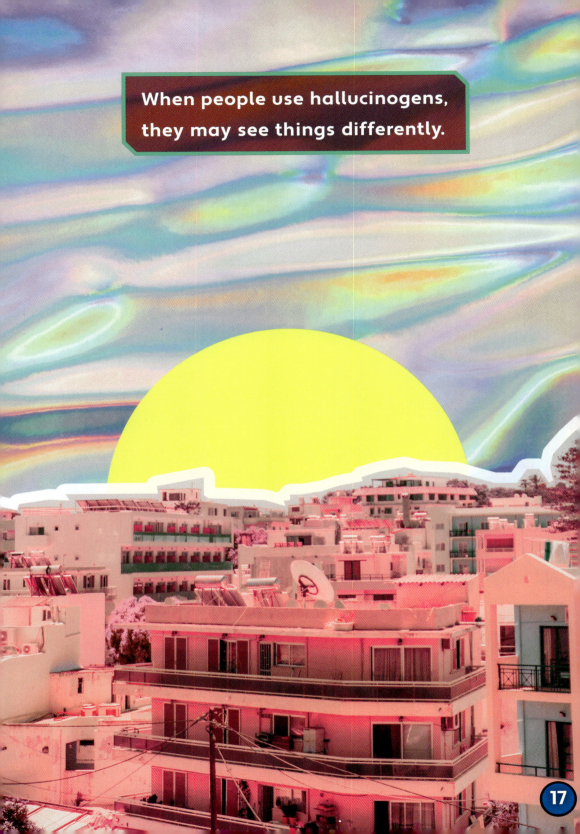

Beyond Use to Abuse

Drugs are meant to be used in specific ways. This is supposed to keep people safe. Using a drug in any other way is called *abuse*. Taking more medicine than prescribed is abuse. So is using medicine meant for someone else. Abusing drugs can put people at risk.

> Using illegal drugs can be especially dangerous. No one checks these drugs for safety. They may be mixed with even more harmful things. This can make people ill. It can even be deadly.

Can't Stop

Most people do not intend to abuse drugs. However, some people develop **addictions**. Their bodies and brains start feeling a strong need for the drugs. This makes it very hard to stop.

Addiction can happen with many drugs. However, some are more addictive than others.

> Because it is legal, it is easier for people to become addicted to alcohol. This is called alcohol abuse disorder, or alcoholism. It becomes hard for people with this addiction to stop drinking.

Opioids are very addictive. Doctors need to work closely with people taking them to help avoid an addiction.

How does addiction work? The human brain creates chemicals that make people feel good. Some drugs cause the brain to make more of these chemicals. Soon, the brain becomes less able to do this on its own. Then, people start to need the drugs to feel good.

People with addictions may stop caring about other things. Sometimes, this leads to actions that can hurt others. They may steal to get money to buy drugs.

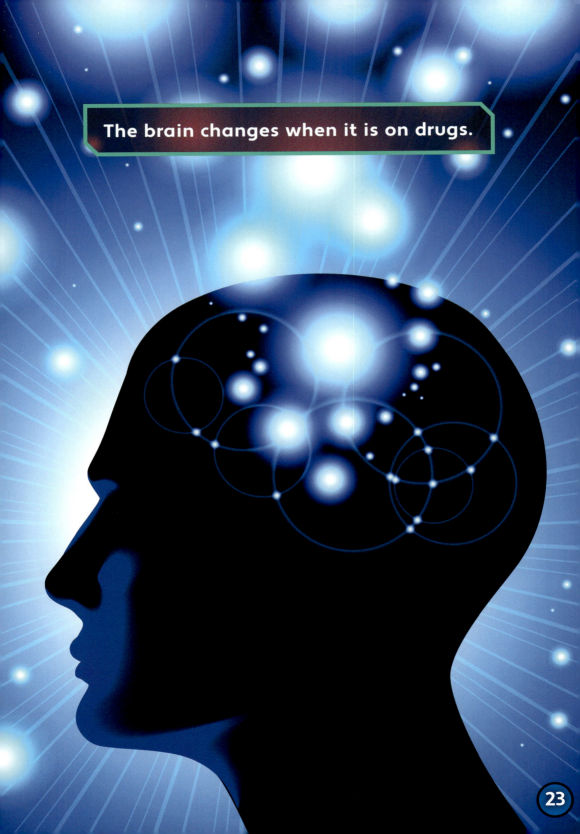

The brain changes when it is on drugs.

Seeking Help

Addiction is an illness. People with addictions can get better. However, they may need help from doctors. Some people go to special places that focus on treating addiction.

There are also peer support groups. This is when many people struggling with addictions get together to help one another.

> If you or someone you know has a drug addiction, talk to a trusted adult. A counselor, family member, or teacher may be able to help.

Staying Healthy

Drugs can help you stay healthy. But it is important to use them as intended. Abusing drugs can lead to short- and long-term damage.

You only have one body. It is your job to take care of it.

Young people are at higher risk of harm from drugs. That's because they are still growing. Damage done to their bodies and brains may never be undone.

Types of Drugs

Different drugs do different things. Review some of the key categories.

Type of Drug	Examples	Intended outcome of use	Effects on the body
Depressants	• Alcohol • Cannabis • Sleep aids	Relaxing the brain and body	• Sleepiness • Slowed breathing and heartbeat • Slower brain function
Stimulants	• Caffeine • Cocaine • Meth	Boosting the brain and body	• Increased breathing and heart rate • Shakiness • Nervousness and anxiety
Opioids	• Pain killers • Fentanyl	Relieving pain	• Pain relief • Sleepiness • Nausea
Hallucinogens	• LSD • Mushrooms	• No legal use • Recreationally used to change one's senses or feelings	• Changed way of seeing the world • A shift in emotions

SilverTips for SUCCESS

★ SilverTips for REVIEW

Review what you've learned. Use the text to help you.

Define key terms

addiction
depressants
hallucinogens
opioids
stimulants

Check for understanding

List some differences between stimulants and depressants.

What does it mean to abuse drugs?

What happens to the body when it has an addiction?

Think deeper

What have you heard from the media about drugs and drug abuse? How accurate do you think that information is?

★ SilverTips on TEST-TAKING

- **Make a study plan.** Ask your teacher what the test is going to cover. Then, set aside time to study a little bit every day.

- **Read all the questions carefully.** Be sure you know what is being asked.

- **Skip any questions** you don't know how to answer right away. Mark them and come back later if you have time.

Glossary

abuse the use of drugs in a way that is not intended

addictions physical and mental needs for things

anxiety strong feelings of worry or fear, especially if the feelings don't go away

illegal against the law

nerves tiny parts of the body that send messages to and from the brain

overdoses taking too much of a drug in a way that often causes harm

prescribe to write a doctor's order for a medical patient

recreationally outside the scope of a prescription use

seizures sudden bursts of electricity in the brain that can cause people to shake or lose consciousness

side effects unexpected or bad result of using medicine or other substances

Read More

Gagne, Tammy. *Teens Dealing with Addiction (Teens Dealing with Adversity).* San Diego, CA: BrightPoint Press, 2025.

Kuehl, Ashley. *Smoking and Vaping (Health: Need to Know).* Minneapolis: Bearport Publishing, 2026.

Wolf, Ryan. *Addictions (Rosen Teen Talk).* New York: Rosen Publishing, 2021.

Learn More Online

1. Go to **FactSurfer.com** or scan the QR code below.
2. Enter "**Drugs and Alcohol**" into the search box.
3. Click on the cover of this book to see a list of websites.

Index

addiction 20–22, 24

alcohol 4, 6, 20, 28

caffeine 12–13, 28

depressants 8, 10, 12, 28

drug abuse 18, 20, 26

fentanyl 14, 28

hallucinogens 16–17, 28

illegal drugs 12, 14, 18

laws 6

opioids 14–15, 21, 28

pain 14, 28

prescriptions 14

stimulants 12, 28

About the Author

Ashley Kuehl is an editor and writer specializing in nonfiction for young people. She lives in Minneapolis, MN.